THE CHEF SAYS

Also available in the
Words of Wisdom series:

The Architect Says
Laura S. Dushkes

The Designer Says
Sara Bader

The Filmmaker Says
Jamie Thompson Stern

the
CHEF
says

Quotes, Quips,
and Words
of Wisdom

compiled & edited by
Nach Waxman & Matt Sartwell

Princeton Architectural Press, New York

Whatever the chef says, the right—the only—answer is, "Yes, chef!"

Veterans of professional kitchens know just how important it is to execute instructions quickly, exactly, and without question. Cooks who forget this find new jobs. Often.

In the midst of service in a busy restaurant, there's no room for a "But!" a "Why?" or a "How about...." The chef speaks, and the cooks act.

Great chefs are not self-effacing, timid, or indecisive. They run a kitchen full of cooks because they have vision and ideas—and the will to direct others in making them concrete. While smart chefs encourage creative input from their brigade, there's no room for discussion at times when the slightest disruption can send an entire restaurant into the weeds.

So it follows that even in quieter moments, what chefs have to say is often crisply opinionated and very illuminating—even if it's not always kind.

Running a bookstore devoted to food and drink means that we deal with chefs and pro cooks all the time. On a daily basis we see just how interested they are in what their colleagues are doing and have done. A rising star on the Lower East Side doesn't necessarily want to make Joel Robuchon's signature potato puree, but encountering another chef's ideas fires the burners of her imagination. She may decide that Robuchon is completely off base and take off running in a completely different direction, but his ideas provide her with a spark.

It is our hope that this volume in Princeton Architectural Press's Words of Wisdom series might serve a similar purpose. We want it to be a spur to the creative thinking processes of cooks and chefs. And with that in mind we offer a few extras— an amuse-bouche, as it were—to demonstrate the way it works. You may not agree with Thomas Keller's sunny assertion that "If I'm happy, then a great percentage of the customers will be happy, too." You may scorn Jeremiah Tower when he says, "Chefs have a reputation for bad behavior, in part because they have to play so hard to counteract the daily pileup of tension and fatigue."

But you might just nod your head at this from legendary New Orleans chef Leah Chase: "You have to be yourself when you are creating and cooking. You do what you need to do and you do it to the best of your ability." At least, it's a place to start thinking.

Nach Waxman and Matt Sartwell

All I ever wanted was a restaurant.

Cindy Pawlcyn (1955–)

I was lucky to have grown
up in a poor family. If I had
been rich, I might have become
a lawyer....But I was poor,
and God made me to be a chef.
I smell like a chef, I feel like
a chef, I look like a chef. I am
chef....I could have been a
millionaire....What a disaster.

Michel Richard (1948–)

WORKING IN THE
KITCHEN IS MY
SOUL AND MY LIFE,
AND I LOVE IT.
I'M NOT THERE
BECAUSE PEOPLE
EXPECT TO SEE ME;
I AM THERE BECAUSE
I WANT TO BE.

Heinz Beck (1963–)

There are many people who claim to be good cooks, just as there are many people who, after having repainted the garden gate, take themselves to be painters.

Fernand Point (1897–1955)

The difference between being a good cook and a good chef is as big as the difference between playing online Texas Hold 'Em in your pajamas and holding a chair at the World Series of Poker.

Gabrielle Hamilton (1965–)

We don't remember
the exact age when
I told my mother
I wanted to be a cook,
but she still keeps
a cooking coat she
made for me when
I was only nine.

Joan Roca (1964–)

MY FATHER CRIED WHEN I SAID I WANTED TO BE A CHEF.

Michael Symon (1969–)

I'M NOT SELF-TAUGHT. I WAS TAUGHT BY A NUMBER OF GREAT CHEFS THROUGHOUT THE YEARS WHO TOOK TIME WITH A SMART-ASS KID.

Hugh Acheson (1971–)

I am self-taught,
and proud of being so.
What I may lack
from not having had
a master to guide me,
I have gained in
enjoying the freedom
to indulge my curiosity.

Raymond Blanc (1949–)

The person who makes the food— his physique, his food, his soul— is unique. It is like fingerprints or handwriting.

Musa Dağdeviren (1960–)

THE FOOD ON THE PLATE
ESTABLISHES A DIALOGUE
WITH ME. ALMOST IMMEDIATELY
I KNOW THE COOK'S AGE, HIS
LEVEL OF CULINARY TRAINING,
HIS EXPOSURE TO CURRENT
REFERENCE POINTS, THE LEVEL
OF PALATE DEVELOPMENT,
SINCERITY, SENSE OF HUMOR,
AND SIZE OF EGO.

Patrick O'Connell (1945-)

If there is a career
which has a lifelong
apprenticeship,
it is certainly ours.

Georges Blanc (1953–)

You need an entire life just to know about tomatoes.

Ferran Adrià (1962–)

THE ART OF COOKING IS PERHAPS ONE OF THE MOST USEFUL FORMS OF DIPLOMACY.

Auguste Escoffier (1846–1935)

I BAKED BREAD FOR THE FIRST TIME TO IMPRESS A GIRL.

Jim Lahey (1966–)

MY MOTHER LIKED TO BAKE. I DON'T. I DON'T DO IT WELL, BECAUSE YOU HAVE TO BE RIGHT ON TARGET. I THINK THAT IS WHERE BAKING AND I FALL APART.

Leah Chase (1923–)

My whole approach is to look in cupboards and throw a bunch of stuff together. It can't really be bad if it's coated in chocolate and butter. Just enjoy yourself.

Christina Tosi (1982–)

There are at least as many different renditions of the "authentic" as there are cooks to provide them.

Paul Bertolli (1953–)

I DON'T DO IT LIKE MAMMA DID IT, BECAUSE MAMMA—JUST BECAUSE SHE DID IT—DIDN'T NECESSARILY DO IT RIGHT.

Michael White (1972–)

TODAY'S INNOVATION IS TOMORROW'S TRADITION.

Lidia Bastianich (1947–)

I'm sometimes
portrayed as
taking a stick
to gastronomic
tradition, but
I believe that what
I'm really doing is
taking up a baton
and running with it.

Heston Blumenthal (1966–)

THE KITCHEN IS AN AWESOME PLAYGROUND. IT'S A PLACE FOR YOU TO EXPERIMENT, TO LOVE, TO TAKE THOSE RISKS, TO PUSH THE BUTTON, TO PUSH THE ENVELOPE. WHAT'S GONNA HAPPEN? IF IT SUCKS, YOU'RE GONNA EAT IT, YOU'RE STILL GONNA EAT IT.

Barbara Lynch (1964–)

You must think like a child with the eyes of a chef, open and naive. Never say something doesn't work or is impossible to do.

Juan Mari Arzak (1942–)

WHEN I LOOK
AT A DISH, I THINK,
WHAT CAN BE
REMOVED WITHOUT
COMPROMISING THE
DISH OR SACRIFICING
FLAVOR? ONLY
WHEN IT'S PARED
DOWN TO ITS ESSENCE
IS IT FINISHED.

David Kinch (1974–)

A salad with too many walnuts or a sauce with too many capers is like a Sunday with too many free hours— you stop appreciating the pleasure they provide. I think about that when I cook. Put just enough sweet cubes of carrots in a soup, and you won't have to search too hard to find one, but when you do, it'll still give you a little thrill.

April Bloomfield (1974–)

I don't believe
in putting a nuance
of ginger in a dish
such that you
can barely taste it.
If you say there is
ginger in the sauce,
you should really
be able to taste it.

Ming Tsai (1964–)

WE TRY TO SMASH YOUR FACE IN WITH FLAVOR. IT'S AS SIMPLE AS THAT.

Sat Bains (1971–)

One of the main points
about the enjoyment
of food and wine seems to
me to lie in having what
you want when you want it
and in the particular
combination you fancy.

Elizabeth David (1913-92)

I cook the food that I want to eat, and it just so happens that other people want to eat it too.

Nancy Silverton (1954–)

When I visualize
a dessert on the plate,
it's an inside-out
experience. I envision
taking a bite of
the dessert—how does
it taste? How does it
feel in the mouth?
The plating comes last,
after I have figured
out the flavor elements.

Emily Luchetti (1957–)

Sometimes I look at the plate and get inspired— it's almost like the shape, color, and finish of the plate is telling me what to cook.

Tadashi Ono (1962–)

To Make the Image of Saint Marthe:...
Make terraces of brown bread, with
a damsel sitting on the terrace, and
with the terrace covered with green tin
leaf strewn with herbs in the likeness
of green grass. You need a lion who
has his two forefeet and head in the
damsel's lap. For him you can make
a brass mouth and a thin brass tongue,
with paper teeth glued to the mouth.
Add some camphor and a little cotton,
and when you would like to present
it before the lords, touch the fire to it.

Taillevent (Guillaume Tirel, ca. 1315–95)

DO NOT FUSS WITH THE NATURAL STATE OF THE FOOD JUST TO SHOW THAT YOU ARE A CLEVER COOK.

Mei Yuan (1716–97)

ALWAYS ENTERTAIN THE POSSIBILITY THAT SOMETHING, NO MATTER HOW SQUIGGLY AND SCARY LOOKING, MIGHT JUST BE GOOD.

Anthony Bourdain (1956–)

The stalked tunicate is
an invasive fouling organism
here but a delicacy in
Korea. We have eaten it,
but it looks like a small
penis and squirts into your
mouth when you bite
into it. This is an example
of a challenging ingredient.

Bun Lai (1971–)

IF AN INGREDIENT IS
INVOLVED IN A DISH, IT'S
BECAUSE ITS PRESENCE
IS ESSENTIAL FOR GIVING
THE DISH MEANING. THERE
IS THEREFORE NO REASON
FOR HAVING AN ARSENAL
OF GARNISHES THAT SERVE
AN INDISTINCT PURPOSE.

Andoni Luis Aduriz (1971–)

Often I will start with one of my trusted recipes, then I open my box of tricks and add sauces, oils, powders, and garnishes, as a child might experiment with building blocks.

Jean-Christophe Novelli (1961–)

First thing in the morning, you'll see me with books in my hands, doing research on my trade.

Cook in *The Man Who Tried to Hide His Face*, by the Greek comic playwright Anaxippus (ca. 303 BC)

When I was twelve,
I decided to become a
chef. I stole a book from
the library about the
greatest restaurants in
France. I'd flip the pages
and dream. I should
return that book to
the library some day. . . .

Eric Ripert (1965–)

AS A RECIPE ADDICT, I CAN NEVER HAVE ENOUGH.

Joyce Goldstein (1935-)

I LEARNED TO COOK IN ORDER TO GET AWAY FROM RECIPES.

Tom Colicchio (1962–)

All of us have,
at one time or another,
salivated over a
picture in a cookbook
and, by dint of hard
work and following
the directions to a T,
turned out something
just a cut above a
braised running shoe.

Gray Kunz (1955–)

A recipe is at the very least a method of accounting for a cooking process. At best, it captures a memory or inspired moment in cooking. But it can never quite tell enough, nor can it thoroughly describe the ecstatic moments when the intuition, skill, and accumulated experience of the book merge with the taste and composition of the food.

Paul Bertolli (1953–)

Everything we do,
no matter what we do,
is about the purity
of the ingredients.
You might take a
pineapple and juice
it and gel it and turn
it into a film, but it
still tastes like a great,
ripe pineapple.

Grant Achatz (1974–)

WHEN YOU GET CLOSE
TO THE RAW MATERIALS
AND TASTE THEM AT THE
MOMENT THEY LET GO
OF THE SOIL, YOU LEARN
TO RESPECT THEM. WE NEVER
ALTER THE RAW MATERIAL
TO SUCH AN EXTENT THAT
WHEN THEY REACH THE
PLATE, THEY NO LONGER
HAVE ANY CONNECTION
WITH THEIR ORIGINS.

René Redzepi (1977–)

Eschew the unnatural and artificial.

Shizuo Tsuji (1933–93)

If you can get past the fact that you're playing God on some level—that I can actually make a turducken that is one solid piece of meat—then why not? If we can agree that it's okay to peel a carrot or boil a potato and mash it, then why not re-form a chicken?

Wylie Dufresne (1970–)

Oh, dearie, dainty doesn't do it in the kitchen.

Julia Child (1912–2004)

WHEN YOU'RE HOLDING
A FORTY-FIVE-POUND
LAMB AS SHE CRIES, AND
YOU SLAUGHTER THAT
ANIMAL, YOU'RE GOING
TO USE EVERY LAST BIT
OF IT BECAUSE YOU WOULD
FEEL LIKE A COMPLETE
ASSHOLE IF YOU DIDN'T.

Chris Cosentino (1972–)

Sometimes, when I look at the way people treat meat inefficiently by neglecting the simpler cuts or just by overindulging in it, I think there should be some kind of driver's license for meat eaters, for which the test would be raising and getting to know an animal, then killing and eating it.

Magnus Nilsson (1983–)

A farm turns out a head on each beautifully well-raised pig, but nobody's rushing to eat it. That's where the cook steps in: you take it, you cook it, you make it delicious. That's the most badass way you can connect with what you cook: elevate it, honor it, lavish it with care and attention— whether you're slicing scallions or spooning up caviar or broiling up half a pig's head.

David Chang (1977–)

With the relatively small number of people I feed, is it really my responsibility to worry about carbon footprint?

Thomas Keller (1955–)

IF I HAVE UNSUSTAINABLE FOODS ON MY MENU THEN I'M A PART OF THE PROBLEM. I CAN'T LIVE WITH THAT. I WANT TO BE PART OF THE SOLUTION.

Ben Shewry (1977–)

Italians walk into every store with the intention of taking home the very best stuff in the store. They think of this as their God-given right and responsibility— not just an option when they feel like splurging.

Mario Batali (1960-)

Parsimony is an excellent source of inspiration.

Mark Best (1969–)

The more I cook,
the more I realize that
a chef should not
shy away from mundane
things like making
a lemon vinaigrette.
A chef should take
pleasure in them.

Marc Vetri (1966–)

I FRET ABOUT SALADS:
WILL I GET A DECENT ONE
OR SOMETHING THROWN
TOGETHER BY A NOVICE?
MOST RESTAURANTS
MISTAKENLY GIVE THE
LEAST-EXPERIENCED COOKS
THE JOB OF DRESSING
A SALAD, A SKILL THAT
TAKES PRACTICE.

David Tanis (1953–)

Nowadays it seems that if you're not involved in certain kitchen trends, you are disqualified before you even begin: you won't be noticed. The pressure to follow a path that is unfamiliar, one that's leading in the wrong direction, can ruin potentially great restaurants and chefs. They take the wrong turn and end up losing both their way and their enthusiasm.

Pedro Subijana (1948-)

I view trends in food like haute couture. From wild, wonderful, and wacky come changes, growth, and evolution.

Sherry Yard (1964–)

I mean, I love
me some bacon,
but if I see bacon
in desserts one
more time or
bacon in a drink…
come on now:
I wanted a beverage,
not breakfast.

Hugh Acheson (1971–)

YOU DON'T WANT A PIECE OF LIVER THAT LOOKS LIKE A COUCH, SO WHY SHOULD YOUR CHOCOLATE CAKE LOOK LIKE A CUCKOO CLOCK?

Wayne Harley Brachman (1947–)

SIMPLE FOOD DOESN'T MEAN SIMPLISTIC. IT REQUIRES A HEALTHY DOSE OF SKILL AND HARD WORK.

Tom Colicchio (1962–)

If you want to
check a pastry chef's
skill at making
ice cream, taste his
or her vanilla ice cream,
because, with
only five ingredients,
it is impossible
to hide any flaws.

Sarabeth Levine (1943–)

When I was young,
I thought it was my job
to always add another
taste dimension to every
ingredient. But these days
I find that approach a little
arrogant. The real work
of a chef is to coax out the
fundamental taste that
is innate to any ingredient.

Yoshihiro Murata (1951–)

WHY DAMAGE OR MASK THE FLAVOR OF FINE MEAT, THE VERDANT FRESHNESS OF SPRING VEGETABLES?

Jean Troisgros (1926–83) and **Pierre Troisgros** (1928–)

GOOD FRESH FOOD IS THE BEST INGREDIENT THAT ANY CHEF COULD ASK FOR.

Ana Sortun (1967–)

JUST BECAUSE TWO
COMPONENTS ARE AMAZING
DOESN'T MEAN THAT
COMBINING THEM WILL
WORK. I HAVE LEARNED
THIS LESSON OVER AND
OVER, USUALLY RIGHT
BEFORE SERVICE BEGINS,
AT WHICH POINT I SPEND
THE REST OF THE NIGHT
MISERABLE BECAUSE
I KNOW WE ARE PRODUCING
LESS THAN OUR BEST.

Daniel Patterson (1969–)

All I need for a good time is a whole pig head, simply roasted, my hands, a lot of napkins, a jar of pickled chilies, and a few friends ready to get elbow deep.

Zakary Pelaccio (1973–)

There is no better accompaniment to pork than pork.

Suzanne Goin (1966–)

Ham held the same rating as the basic black dress. If you had a ham in the meat house any situation could be faced.

Edna Lewis (1916–2006)

HAM ISN'T WHAT IT USED TO BE.

James Beard (1903-85)

SOMETHING MAGICAL
HAPPENS WHEN FOOD IS
COOKING—THE REST OF
THE WORLD MELTS AWAY,
AND NOTHING EXISTS EXCEPT
WHAT'S IN THE SKILLET
IN FRONT OF YOU—AND IT
TALKS, BREATHES, AND LIVES.
THE SOUNDS, AROMAS,
TEXTURES, FLAVORS, AND
THE HEAT OF THE KITCHEN—
EVEN THE OCCASIONAL
SEARING BURN—FEEL GOOD.

Donald Link (1969-)

Even after all this time in the kitchen, I still love watching garlic go nutty in hot fat or peeking underneath a piece of caramelizing fennel to see it browning and growing sweeter by the minute.
I love spooning pan liquid over roasting meat, piling any vegetable matter on top, and gently smooshing it. And as many livers as I've seared in my life, the smell of one meeting a hot pan still makes my knees tremble. The small delights are the most lovely.

April Bloomfield (1974–)

Butter! Give me butter! Always butter!

Fernand Point (1897–1955)

BUTTER, DUDE. BUTTER!

Matthew Gaudet (1971–)

There are hazards to cooking.

Anita Lo (1965–)

REMEMBER, IT IS NEVER THE KNIFE'S FAULT.

Daniel Boulud (1955–)

If I ever get the right material and a kitchen set up how I want it, you'll see a replay...of what happened in the old days with the Sirens. The smell simply won't let anyone get past the alleyway here. Whoever passes by will immediately come to a stop beside the door—struck dumb, nailed to the spot....

Cook in *Brothers*, by the Greek comic playwright Hegesippus (ca. 180 BC)

THE COOK...ALWAYS SEES
THE SAME FOUR WALLS
COVERED WITH COPPER POTS,
WHOSE REFLECTION MAKES
HIM LOSE HIS SIGHT; ADD
TO THIS THE STRESS HE SUFFERS
FROM DEMANDING AND
DIFFICULT WORK AND THEN
THE POISONOUS GAS FROM
THE CHARCOAL BRAZIERS,
WHICH HE BREATHES EVERY
MOMENT OF THE DAY. THIS IS
THE LIFE OF THE COOK.

Antonin Carême (1784–1833)

If you're in our world—
the restaurant business—
you have to be so ready for
a typical Saturday night,
where you have 350 people
coming through the door,
a dish washer doesn't show
up, the drain in the kitchen
backs up, you have a line
cook who cuts her hand
and has to go to the hospital.
That is a typical night.

Susan Feniger (1953–)

You ask why we do it? The burns,
the shouting, the early mornings, the
very late nights, the awkward customer,
the stress, the paranoia, the bullshit,
the sixteen-hour days, the seven days
a week, the nine weeks in a row, the low
wages, the graft....It's because of
this that we do it, and the great staff,
the loyal and happy customers, the new
flavors, the new ideas, the simplicity,
the complexity, the adrenalin, the feeling
of achievement. And above all, I do it
because I love food and booze, and I'm
the luckiest man in the world!

Tom Kerridge (1973-)

IF YOU REALLY LOVE
TO COOK AND THINK THAT
YOU MIGHT LIKE TO DO
IT IN A RESTAURANT OF
YOUR OWN SOMEDAY, HERE'S
MY ADVICE: STAY HOME.
HAVE YOUR FRIENDS OVER
FOR DINNER AND GO NUTS.
BUT KEEP OUT OF THE
RESTAURANT BUSINESS.

Charles Phan (1962–)

Opening a restaurant is the worst feeling in the world. When you open a restaurant, you live it, you sleep it. You always have sawdust on your clothes. You can't shower the smell of the place off you.

David Chang (1977–)

WHEN YOU SET OUT TO CREATE A RESTAURANT, YOU'RE NOT DOING IT FOR FAME IN A GUIDE, PROBABLY NOT EVEN FOR THE CUSTOMERS, BUT FOR YOURSELF.

Neil Perry (1957–)

You can't forget that you cook for customers. If you don't have customers, you close.

Andre Soltner (1932–)

My dream restaurant would be a counter with ten seats. I would cook for you, and then serve you, and then do the dishes. Once you delegate, it doesn't matter how many restaurants you do.

Jean-Georges Vongerichten (1957–)

If you are a chef
and you own your
own restaurant,
it is sometimes more
difficult to make
money because you
are so passionate
about what you do.

Tom Valenti (1959–)

WHEN I WAS YOUNG THERE WERE
CHEFS THAT I ADMIRED, AND AS I GREW
OLDER AND MORE EXPERIENCED IN
MY COOKING I SAW THAT THOSE CHEFS
WEREN'T CHANGING ANYTHING.
I BEGAN TO LOSE RESPECT FOR THEM.
I DON'T WANT TO BE THE GUY THAT
YOUNG CHEFS USED TO LIKE, AND THEN
THEY THINK, "OH YEAH, HE'S JUST
WASHED UP NOW." ACTUALLY, I'D RATHER
BURN OUT THAN BE THAT PERSON.

Ben Shewry (1977–)

A restaurant is changing all the time, and if it's not hungry to move forward, it gets stale.

Michael Anthony (1968–)

TRAVEL BROADENS THE
MIND AND INCREASES
THE POSSIBILITY OF
INSPIRATION. THE TRICK
IS TO IMPORT THESE
IDEAS IN A MATURE WAY
AND INTEGRATE THEM
INTO YOUR OTHER WORK.
A MENU SHOULDN'T
READ LIKE AN ATLAS.

Mark Best (1969–)

WHEN TOO MANY CUISINES ARE REPRESENTED ON A PLATE, YOU'RE NOWHERE.

Peter Hoffman (1956–)

ABOVE ALL, MY CUSTOMERS MUST BE PLEASED, FOR THEY TRUST US IN COMING HERE, AND WE DO NOT HAVE THE RIGHT TO DISAPPOINT THEM.

Frédy Girardet (1936–)

If you haven't planned well enough to be on time and haven't had the decency to call and tell us, you can dine elsewhere.

Magnus Nilsson (1983–)

THERE ARE GREAT
RESTAURANTS, GOOD
RESTAURANTS, AND
POOR RESTAURANTS,
BUT NO RESTAURANT
IS ANY BETTER THAN
THE PERFORMANCE YOU
CAN EXACT FROM IT
BY KNOWING THE CHEF,
THE MAÎTRE D'HÔTEL,
OR THE OWNER.

James Beard (1903–85)

The customer who comes here once or twice a week is a celebrity to us.

Mark Peel (1955–)

There are people who expect you to come out every time, no matter how busy you are, even though you're a guy short in the kitchen and you can't leave.

Bill Telepan (1966–)

PEOPLE STILL COME HERE AND EXPECT A THREE-COURSE MEAL IN AN HOUR. WHAT DO THEY THINK I DO— PULL RABBITS OUT OF A FUCKING HAT? I'M NOT A MAGICIAN.

Marco Pierre White (1961–)

A customer is a friend. Whatever they want in my restaurant they can have.

Tetsuya Wakuda (1959–)

Why am I going to give you a menu? I made the food. Why are you picking?

Mario Carbone (1980–)

You either make the food right or you don't.

Daniel Boulud (1955–)

THE DAY YOU RELAX IS THE DAY THAT IT'S ALL GOING TO CRUMBLE.

Tom Kitchin (1978–)

FEAR MAKES YOU DEVELOP. IT IS CRUCIAL TO THE CREATIVE PROCESS.

Ferran Adrià (1962–)

I LOVE FEELING SCARED. IT MAKES THE WHISKEY TASTE BETTER AT THE END OF THE NIGHT.

Sean Brock (1978–)

A good drink helps to alleviate stress and numbs you to the trivial concerns of a broken society—and to any possible burns or cuts that occur as a result of cooking drunk.

Zakary Pelaccio (1973-)

I LIKE TO START MY DAY OFF WITH A GLASS OF CHAMPAGNE. I LIKE TO WIND IT UP WITH CHAMPAGNE, TOO. TO BE FRANK, I ALSO LIKE A GLASS OR TWO IN BETWEEN.

Fernand Point (1897–1955)

MY GO-TO DRINK AT THE END OF THE NIGHT IS AN ICE-COLD BEER. A CUP OF EARL GREY WITH A SPLASH OF MILK ALSO HITS THE SPOT.

Patricia Yeo (1959–)

There's not a day that doesn't pass that I don't have a couple of Diet Pepsis. That's usually my nightcap. I know it sounds crazy, but when I come home from working and everyone's sleeping, there's nothing like a little Diet Pepsi and the eleven o'clock news.

Michael White (1972–)

If you have a nice, serene, happy environment where your cooks are calm, I believe that it affects the food and everything turns out better.

Emma Hearst (1986–)

I have fired people who can't suffer their setbacks and petty failures. If they go down early and spend the rest of their five-hour shift that way, it threatens to sink the whole boat, and that can't happen just because you burned your first omelette and had to refire it. You've got to get your GI Jane on.

Gabrielle Hamilton (1966)

I have a streak of obstinacy that often drives my chefs crazy, but has proved useful in the kitchen: I don't take the easy route and I don't give up.

Heston Blumenthal (1966–)

Well, one day recently my girlfriend
told me that the night before we had a
conversation in my sleep. I said, "No, I sleep
like a log, never talk in my sleep." "Well,"
she said, "last night I felt you poking me
in the small of my back. I turned around,
thinking, 'Oh, he wants to get frisky,'
only to see you brushing my bottom with
your finger like you were reading a book.
I said, 'What are you doing?' and you
replied, 'Looking for a lamb recipe.'"

André Garrett (1972–)

ALL THROUGH HIGH
SCHOOL AND COLLEGE
I WORKED IN RESTAURANTS
AND FELL IN LOVE WITH
RESTAURANT PEOPLE.
IT WAS A BIT LIKE BELONGING
TO A CIRCUS. THEY WERE
SO ECCENTRIC AND
UNUSUAL AND FASCINATING.
AND ABNORMAL.

Patrick O'Connell (1945–)

Cooks are a crafty, nonconformist crowd, more so even than waiters, though both are unstable, irresponsible, and often downright infamous.

Nicolas Freeling (1927–2003)

Introductions are awkward, especially in kitchens. Everyone's sizing each other up, and no one wants to take the time to learn your name until you've been to the battle of dinner service enough nights in a row to show that you aren't going anywhere.

Christina Tosi (1982–)

About five years ago I was in the locker room putting on my whites to start the day. I was standing next to a new stagiaire, who was also changing. He looked over at me and said excitedly, "So, what do you do around here?" I was caught off guard but replied, "I'm the chef." He said, "Oh," and that was the last time we ever spoke.

Wylie Dufresne (1970–)

ALWAYS KEEP YOUR DOOR OPEN TO STAFF AND TREAT THEM LIKE FAMILY.

Ming Tsai (1964–)

The food was perfect or it was wrong; failure was never an option; and "Yes, chef" was the only proper response to any request.

Grant Achatz (1974–)

The kitchen—which in my experience is staffed by an extraordinarily diverse group of people who become an incredibly close team when dressed in the whites, inhabit a fairly inhospitable space, and produce delicious food on time at different times— is the heart of a restaurant.

Fergus Henderson (1963–)

EVERY KITCHEN WILL
HAVE TENSION IN IT....
IT'S THE NATURE OF THE
BEAST. IT'S HOT. IT'S STEAMY.
YOU'VE GOT CUSTOMERS
WHO ARE DEMANDING AND
CHANNELING THAT DEMAND
THROUGH THE WAITERS,
AND THE WAITERS ARE
UNDERSTANDABLY TENSE
BECAUSE THEY HAVE
TO PRODUCE THE GOODS.

Sally Clarke (1954–)

You can take someone, and train them, and show them something, and all of a sudden they turn around and they know how to do it better than you do, and you go, "Oh! That's what I really wanted to do in the first fucking place."

Waldy Malouf (1953–)

TECHNIQUES ARE NOT THE MOST DIFFICULT TO TEACH. THE ATTITUDES CHEFS TAKE ARE MUCH MORE IMPORTANT.

Alain Ducasse (1956–)

YOU WILL NOT LOSE YOUR HEAD. YOU WILL NOT RUN YOUR AREA OF OPERATIONS...INTO A CHAOTIC TRAIN WRECK. YOU WILL LEARN TO PRIORITIZE TASKS LIKE A COLD-BLOODED PROFESSIONAL...SO THAT FINAL ASSEMBLY, OR "PICK-UP," WILL NOT SEND YOU INTO GIBBERING PARALYSIS.

Anthony Bourdain (1956–)

Watching an organized, disciplined, busy kitchen in full swing is a graceful thing, while the horror of watching a kitchen go down full flight is more like a B-grade Hollywood bloodfest.

Andrew McConnell (1969–)

You know that old expression "It's not whether you win or lose; it's how you play the game." That line was definitely not coined by a chef. Because for a chef, it's only about whether or not you pull through. If you fail, nobody cares how hard you tried.

Marcus Samuelsson (1970–)

I am well aware that a chef is only as good as his last meal.

Gordon Ramsay (1966–)

The difference between
what is good, very good,
and exceptional can be found
in repetition. A chef must
master the basics before he can
create something that is truly
exceptional, and the only way
to master something is to
repeat the process many times,
honing your skills and making
slight changes to your methods
until you have reached your
own version of perfection.

Alex Atala (1968–)

I COOKED SCALLOPS THE OTHER NIGHT, MAYBE FIFTY TIMES, AND EACH TIME IT WAS DIFFERENT. THERE WAS PROBABLY ONE PERSON THERE AT THE END THAT GOT THE PERFECT SCALLOP DISH.

Alice Waters (1944–)

I used to pass my sauces through a food mill. Fuck that! Some food is too labor-intensive.

Einat Admony (1971–)

I HAVE A RULE IN MY KITCHEN THAT IF IT TAKES TOO LONG, IT'S NOT WORTH DOING. WE ARE FEEDING PEOPLE. YOU CAN'T AFFORD TO SPEND TOO MUCH TIME ON THE PLATE.

Nico Ladenis (1934–)

As a chef you are likely to feel a lot of pressure, working from early morning to late at night and not really getting paid for it, but you keep doing it because you love it. You feel nobody understands you, and tattoos are one of the ways you try and communicate with the world outside, saying "I'm a chef. I'm a badass!"

Kobe Desramaults (1980-)

When I am working in the kitchen, I never wear a toque.... It is something I find slightly pretentious....I feel the same way over the more recent custom of embroidering chefs' names on their jackets....
I find it ridiculous and more than unnecessary to have my own name written on me as though I were a packet of cheese.

Pierre Koffmann (1948–)

I worry that once you get known for one thing, you're never really allowed to try another.

Alex Stupak (1980–)

Once you've got three stars, there's no turning back. You've just got to keep going.

Juan Mari Arzak (1942–)

I myself learned to cook so beautifully in Sicily that I sometimes make the dinner guests gnaw on the cookpot because they like the food so much.

Cook in *The All-Night Festival*, by the Greek comic playwright Alexis (ca. 350 BC)

VANITY IS AN ESTABLISHED TRADITION AMONG COOKS.

Michael Roberts (1949–2005)

EVERY CHEF HAS
A LOVE-HATE DISH,
THE DISH THAT MADE
IT INTO THE FIRST
REVIEW, THE ONE THAT
CUSTOMERS CALL
AHEAD FOR, THE DISH,
THEREFORE, THE CHEF
WILL NEVER BE ABLE
TO TAKE OFF THE MENU.

Suzanne Goin (1966–)

There's something kind of satisfying in killing a dish that's really popular. Not because it's sadistic, but because I got that to be as good as I'm interested in its being, and keeping things on the menu that are giving you a hard time or that are more problematic or that you aren't completely happy with gives you another chance to make it better every day. But once you have it to a place that you really, really love it, cooking it becomes pretty boring.

Andrea Reusing (1968-)

I mean, *who* understands them— food critics? I don't.

Nico Ladenis (1934–)

The critic is important, but you know what's also important? The lady sitting next to the critic who might tell her friends or come back next week.

Peter Hoffman (1956–)

THERE IS NOTHING MORE
TEDIOUS THAN AN EVENING
SPENT DISCUSSING EVERY
DISH EATEN IN MINUTE DETAIL.
"OH, DAPHNE, HOW DID
YOU MANAGE TO INSERT
THOSE CARROTS IN YOUR
HOLLOWED-OUT ZUCCHINI?"

Simon Hopkinson (1954–)

We make fucking food. We aren't saving people's lives here.

Sat Bains (1971–)

Chefs are not supposed to be celebrities! We smell bad, we're adrenaline junkies, and we have strange social habits!

Patricia Yeo (1959–)

IT'S BETTER TO BE CALLED A CUNT THAN BE IGNORED.

Marco Pierre White (1961–)

Sometimes I feel like I am an animal in a zoo and I need to hide out in the kitchen.

Frank Stitt (1954–)

I didn't have a strong sense of belonging in the world, but I found that in the kitchen.

Richard Blais (1972–)

THIS IS THE
GREAT CHALLENGE:
TO MAINTAIN PASSION
FOR THE EVERYDAY
ROUTINE AND THE
ENDLESSLY REPEATED
ACT, TO DERIVE
DEEP GRATIFICATION
FROM THE MUNDANE.

Thomas Keller (1955–)

When your timing is right, your vision narrows. Time collapses, and you exist in an eternal now with no past and no future. It may just be a kitchen, but when our timing is right, we transcend time and space.

Amanda Cohen (1975–)

CLEAN PLATES DON'T LIE.

Dan Barber (1969–)

INDEX

We must begin by acknowledging each of the chefs we've cited—and all the other pros whose smart, sharp, funny words did not make the final list. The restaurant business brings out passion in people: we found many hundreds more great quotes than this book contains. The hard work lay in choosing what to exclude, given the book's size, not in finding things to consider.

Helen Johnston and Jennifer Hughes, our able coworkers at Kitchen Arts & Letters, were enormously helpful in suggesting people to consider, gathering material, and providing thoughtful insights. Thanks, too, to Maron Waxman for some very helpful research.

We're glad that Rob Shaeffer thought of us for this project and put us in touch with Princeton Architectural Press in the form of Sara Bader, whose deft skill at suggesting how to organize our work was matched by her patience with a couple of former book editors who thought they knew how everything should happen. Sara Stemen showed the same resilience as we were making the final cuts and matching quotes for each spread of the book.

And thanks also belong to the customers who have supported our store over the years in which independent booksellers have become an endangered species. We wouldn't have served such a specialized market for more than thirty years if it weren't for our own regulars. We're very glad to have them.

Published by
Princeton Architectural Press
37 East Seventh Street
New York, New York 10003

Visit our website at www.papress.com.

Printed and bound in China by C&C Offset
17 16 15 14   4 3 2 1 First edition

Developmental editor: Sara Bader
Project editor: Sara Stemen
Designer: Elana Schlenker
Series designer: Paul Wagner

Special thanks to:
Mariam Aldhahi, Meredith Baber, Sara Bader, Nicola Bednarek Brower, Janet
Behning, Megan Carey, Carina Cha, Andrea Chlad, Barbara Darko, Benjamin
English, Russell Fernandez, Will Foster, Jan Hartman, Jan Haux, Diane Levinson,
Jennifer Lippert, Katharine Myers, Jaime Nelson, Jay Sacher, Rob Shaeffer,
Marielle Suba, Kaymar Thomas, and Joseph Weston of Princeton Architectural Press
—Kevin C. Lippert, publisher

Library of Congress Cataloging-in-Publication Data
The chef says : quotes, quips, and words of wisdom / compiled and edited by
Nach Waxman and Matt Sartwell.
    pages cm. — (Words of wisdom)
ISBN 978-1-61689-249-4 (alk. paper)
1. Food—Quotations, maxims, etc. 2. Cooking—Quotations, maxims, etc.
I. Waxman, Nach, editor of compilation. II. Sartwell, Matt, editor of compilation.
PN6084.F6.C63 2014
641.5—dc23
                                                              2013049344

IF I STOP COOKING, I'LL DIE.

Michel Bras (1946–)